EATING HEALTH WITH **DR. FRANCIS**

VEGAN
Snacks & Smoothies
Made Simple

Dr. A. Francis

November | 2022

ISBN 979-8-9870220-6-1

t.c.paskpublishing@gmail.com

CONTENTS

Smoothies

Snacks

BREAKFAST IDEA
Vanilla Smoothie

 Rolled oats, ⅓ cup

 Cashew nuts, ½ cup

 Water, 1 cup

 Ripe banana, 1 large

 Vanilla extract, ½ tsp

 Pitted dates, 5 pcs

 Blend all the ingredients in a blender until they blend into a smooth paste.

GREEN ENERGY
Cucumber Smoothie

 Strawberries, ½ cup

 Cucumber, ½ cup

 Kale, 1 cup

 Frozen banana, 1 large

 Almond milk, 1 cup

 Baby spinach, 1 handful

 Blend all the ingredients in a blender until they blend into a smooth paste.

INTEGRAL ~HEALING~

ANTI-INFLAMMATORY
Pineapple Smoothie

 Frozen banana, 1 large

 Almond milk, ½ cup

 Pineapple, 2 cups

 Turmeric powder, ½ tsp

 Ground cinnamon, ¼ tsp

 Ginger (grated), ½ tsp

 Blend all the ingredients in a blender until they blend into a smooth paste.

 MINDFUL WELLNESS

CHOCOLATE
Cherry Smoothie

 Cacao powder, 1 tbsp

 Frozen cherries, 2 cups

 Almond butter, 4 tbsp

 **Frozen banana,** 1 medium

 Protein powder, 1 scoop

 Almond milk, 1 cup

 Spinach, 2 cups

 Blend all ingredients until smooth.

GREEN SPIRULINA
Smoothie Bowl

 Avocado,
1 medium

 Bananas,
2 medium

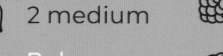 Raspberries,
¾ cup

 Almond
milk,
1 cup

 Baby
spinach,
1 cup

 Spirulina
powder,
1 tsp

 Blend all ingredients until smooth.

CREAMY MINTY
Avocado Smoothie

 Mint leaves, ¼ cup

 Water, ½ cup

 Pitted dates, 2 pcs

 Avocado, 1 medium

 Raw almonds, ⅓ cup

NATURAL VEGAN

 Blend all ingredients until smooth.

Buckwheat Smoothie

 Carrots,
¼ cup

 Kale,
1 cup

 Zucchini,
½ cup

 Green
grapes,
⅓ cup

 Lemon
juice,
1 tbsp

 Hemp
milk,
1 cup

 Buckwheat (soaked),
¼ cup

 Blend all ingredients until
smooth.

IMMUNE-BOOSTING
Lemon Smoothie

 Pineapple, ½ cup

 Peaches, 1 cup

 Chia seeds, 1 tbsp

 Lemon (juiced), 1 large

 Almond milk, 1 cup

 Ginger (grated), ½ tsp

 Blend it all together in a blender until smooth. Enjoy!

MIXED BERRY ENERGIZING
Smoothie Bowl

 Beet (peeled), 1 medium

 Pitted dates, 2 pcs

 Chia seeds, 1 tbsp

 Mixed berries (frozen), 1½ cup

 Almond milk, ½ cup

 Baby spinach, 1 cup

 Blend it all together and serve with fresh berries, bananas & seeds

BRAIN POWER
Kale Berry Smoothie

 Blueberries, 1 cup

 Kale, ½ cup

 Chia seeds, 1 tbsp

 Frozen banana, 1 medium

 Almond butter, 1 tbsp

 Almond milk, 1½ cup

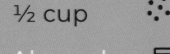

 Blend it all together in a blender until smooth. Enjoy!

MINDFUL WELLNESS

MANGO & MINT
Refreshing Smoothie

 Mango chunks, 1 cup

 Coconut water, ½ cup

 Lime juice (opt.), 1 tsp

 Coconut milk, ½ cup

 Banana, 1 large

 Mint, 8 leaves

 Blend it all together in a blender until smooth. Enjoy!

LOW CALORIE
Swiss chard Smoothie

 Water, 2 cups

 Apple, 1 medium

 Cucumber, 1 mini

 Swiss chard, 1 cup

 Ginger (grated), 1 tsp

 Lemon (juiced), ½ piece

 Blend it all together in a blender until smooth. Enjoy!

SUPER GREEN

Spirulina Smoothie

 Cucumber,
1 small

 Spinach,
1 handful

 Water,
1 cup

 Ginger,
0.5 inch

 Spirulina powder,
1 tsp

 Apple,
1 medium

 Frozen pineapple,
¾ cup, chunks

 Blend it all together and serve with fresh
berries, bananas & seeds.

SIMPLE AND HEALTHY
Chocolate Smoothie

 Almond milk, 1 cup

 Pitted dates, 2 pcs

 Cacao powder, 2 tbsp

 Frozen bananas, 3 medium

 Vanilla extract, ¼ tsp

 Blend all ingredients until smooth.

COCONUT & MANGO
Creamy Smoothie

 Coconut flakes,
¼ cup

 Coconut milk,
½ cup

 Mango,
1 large

 Cold water,
½ cup

 Ripe banana,
1 large

 Blend it all together in a blender until smooth. Enjoy!

POWER BREAKFAST
Spinach Smoothie

 Peanut butter,
2 tbsp

 Protein powder (opt.),
1 scoop

 Pumpkin seeds,
1 tbsp

 Almond milk,
1 cup

 Baby spinach,
1 cup

 Banana,
1 medium

 Blend it all together in a until smooth. Enjoy!

KALE & APPLE
Green Smoothie

 Chilled water, 1 cup

 Kale, 1 cup

 Lime juice, 1 tbsp

 Green apple, 1 medium

 Cilantro, 1 handful

 Pineapple, ½ cup

 Ginger, ½ inch

 Blend it all together in a blender until smooth. Enjoy!

BERRY BEET
Smoothie Bowl

 Blueberries,
1 cup

 Frozen banana,
1 medium

 Almond milk,
½ cup

 Beet (peeled),
1 small

 Blend and serve with blueberries, chia seeds
or strawberries.

INTEGRAL HEALING

IMMUNE-BOOSTING
Hemp Smoothie

 Lemon (juiced),
1 large

 Ginger (grated),
1 tsp

 Pineapple,
½ cup

 Almond milk,
1 cup

 Peaches,
1 cup

 Hemp seeds,
2 tbsp

 Blend all ingredients until smooth.

INTEGRAL ~ HEALING

VERY BERRY
Beet Smoothie

 Strawberries,
⅓ cup

 Frozen banana,
1 medium

 Blueberries,
1 cup

 Almond milk,
1 cup

 Kale,
½ cup

 Beet,
1 small

 Blend all ingredients until smooth.

BANANA & SPINACH
Energy Smoothie

 Almond milk, 1 cup

 Baby spinach, 1 cup

 Pumpkin seeds, 1 tbsp

 Nut butter, 1 tbsp

 Banana, 1 medium

 Blend all ingredients until smooth.

KALE & SPIRULINA
Smoothie Bowl

 Frozen bananas, 2 medium

 Almond milk, 1 cup

 Spirulina powder, 1 tsp

 Almond butter, 1 tbsp

 Kale, 1 cup

 Pitted dates, 2 pcs

 Blend and serve with berries and chia seeds.

FLAX & CHIA SEED
Brown Rice Crackers

 Flax seeds, 2 tbsp

 Water, ⅓ cup

 Coconut oil, 2 tbsp

 Chia seeds, 1 tbsp

 Salt, ½ tsp

 Brown rice flour, 1 cup

- Mix together the dry ingredients. Add wet ingredients and form a dough; Roll the dough until it is thin;
- Cut the rolled-out dough into desired shapes;
- Bake for 20 min at 350°F (180°C).

HEALTHY SNACK
No Bake Oat Bars

 Cranberries, 2 tbsp

 Peanut butter, ½ cup

 Vanilla extract, 1 tsp

 Rolled oats, 1½ cup

 Maple syrup, ½ cup

- Mix all the ingredients, spread on pan;
- Place in refrigerator until set.

GLUTEN-FREE
Almond Cookies

 Almond flour, 100 g

 Baking soda, ⅓ tsp

 Apple cider vinegar *(or lemon juice),* 1 tsp

 Pitted dates, 4-7 pcs

 Almond milk, 4 tbsp

 Rice flour, 30 g

 Coconut oil, 2 tbsp

 +

- Combine all ingredients in a food processor, roll cookie dough into balls and flatten slightly;
- Bake at 350°F (180°C) for 15-20 minutes.

CASSAVA FLOUR
Blueberry Muffins

 Cassava flour, 2 cups

 Baking powder, 2 tsp

 Apple cider vinegar, 2 tbsp

 Almond milk, 1 cup

 Maple syrup, ⅓ cup

 Blueberries, 1 cup

 Coconut oil, ¼ cup

 Applesauce, ¼ cup

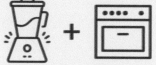

- Mix together the wet ingredients. Add baking powder and mix. Add cassava flour and blueberries, mix;
- Use muffin tin. Pour the batter into each of muffin hole;
- Bake for 25 min at 350°F (180°C).

PROTEIN SNACK
Fudge Brownie Bars

 Black beans,
1½ cups

 Cocoa powder,
3 tbsp

 Maple syrup,
⅓ cup

 Coconut oil,
4 tbsp

 Vanilla extract,
1 tsp

 Baking powder,
½ tsp

- Combine all ingredients in a food processor, spread on baking sheet;
- Bake for 15-20 minutes at 350°F (180°C).

HEALTHY NO-BAKE SNACK
Coffee Energy Bites

 Peanut butter, 1 cup

 Cocoa powder, 2 tbsp

 Rolled oats, 1¾ cup

 Vanilla extract, 1 tsp

 Maple syrup, ½ cup

 Instant coffee, 1 tsp

- Blend all ingredients in food processor until mixture comes together;
- Shape mixture into small balls. Refrigerate for 1 hour.

AVOCADO & CACAO
Chocolate Truffles

 Cacao powder, 2 tbsp

 Coconut flour, 1 tbsp

 Avocado, 1 medium

 Peanut butter, 2 tbsp

 Pitted dates, 5 pcs

- Blend all ingredients. Roll into balls;
- Refrigerate for 1 hour before serving.

PROTEIN SNACKS
Chocolate Balls

 Cacao powder, 2 tbsp

 Rolled oats, 1 cup

 Protein powder, 1 scoop

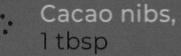 Cacao nibs, 1 tbsp

 Pitted dates, 15 pcs

 +

- Blend all ingredients in food processor until mixture comes together. Shape mixture into small balls.
- Refrigerate for 1 hour before serving.

HEALTHY SNACK IDEAS
Roasted Chickpeas

 Soaked chickpeas
(Soak on room temperature for 8 hrs),
1 cup

 Nutritional yeast,
1 tbsp

Coconut oil,
1 tsp

– SPICES: –

 Black pepper,
¼ tsp

 Onion powder,
¼ tsp

 Turmeric,
¼ tsp

 Himalayan salt,
¼ tsp

 Garlic powder,
¼ tsp

- Preheat oven to 400°F (200°C);
- Spread chickpeas with spices on a baking sheet in one layer;
- Let chickpeas roast from 45 to 55 minutes.

GOJI BERRY
Granola Bars

 Rolled oats, 1 cup

 Goji berries, ¼ cup

 Chopped almonds, ½ cup

 Pitted dates, ½ cup

 Nut butter, ¼ cup

 Maple syrup, ¼ cup

- Combine all ingredients in a food processor, spread on baking sheet;
- Bake at 350°F (180°C) for 15-20 minutes.

4-INGREDIENT
Coconut Cookies

 Coconut flour,
2 cups

 Tapioca (opt.),
3 tbsp

 Ripe bananas,
3 medium

 Raisins (opt.),
2 tbsp

- Combine all the ingredients in a food processor;
- Roll cookie dough into small balls and flatten slightly;
- Bake at 350°F (180°C) for 20 min.

GLUTEN-FREE
Cassava Crackers

 Rosemary (minced), 1 tsp

 Olive oil, 6 tbsp

 Cassava flour, 1 cup

 Salt, ½ tsp

 Garlic powder, ½ tsp

 Water, 8 tbsp

- Mix together the dry ingredients. Add wet ingredients and form a dough; Roll the dough until it is thin;
- Cut the rolled-out dough into desired shapes;
- Bake for 40-50 min at 300°F (150°C)

APPLESAUCE
Peanut Cookies

 Peanut butter,
½ cup

 Maple syrup,
2 tbsp

 Apple sauce
(unsweetened),
¼ cup

 Baking powder,
½ tsp

 Cacao nibs,
2 tbsp

 Oat flour,
1 cup

 +

- Combine all the ingredients in a food processor:
- Roll cookie dough into balls and flatten slightly;
- Bake for 15 min at 350°F (180°C).

EASY ALMOND
Hemp Energy Bites

 Raw cacao powder,
1 tbsp

 Chopped almonds,
2 tbsp

 Almond flour,
¾ cup

 Cinnamon,
½ tsp

 Pitted dates,
1 cup

 Hemp seeds,
3 tbsp

- Blend all ingredients in food processor until mixture comes together. Shape mixture into small balls;
- Refrigerate for 1 hour before serving.

QUICK AND EASY
Chocolate Cupcakes

 Cacao powder,
4 tbsp

 Coconut cream,
10 tbsp

 Pitted dates,
8-10 pcs

 Baking soda,
⅓ tsp

 Rice flour,
5 tbsp

 Cacao nibs,
1 tbsp

- Combine all the ingredients in a blender;
- Use muffin tin. Pour the batter into each of muffin hole;
- Bake for 20 minutes at 375°F (190°C).

OVEN BAKED
Sweet Potato Fries

 Sweet potatoes, 3 pcs

 Smoked paprika, 2 tsp

 Nutritional yeast, 2 tbsp

 Garlic powder, 1 tsp

- Peel and cut the sweet potatoes into strips;
- Add spices and mix;
- Bake at 400°F (200°C) for 30 min.

Hemp Falafel

 Cooked chickpeas, 2 cups

 Himalayan salt, ¼ tsp

Nutritional yeast, 2 tbsp

 Garlic, 2 cloves

 Hemp seeds, 4 tbsp

 + Blend all ingredients in food processor until mixture comes together. Shape mixture into balls. Bake for 20-25 min at 400°F (200°C).

FROZEN CHOCOLATE
Banana Fudge

 Cacao powder, 4 tbsp

 Bananas, 6 medium

 Coconut oil, 6 tbsp

 +

- Blend all ingredients;
- Pour into the mold;
- Place into the freezer overnight.

PEANUT BUTTER
Energy Bites

 Vanilla extract, 1 tsp

 Peanut butter, 1 cup

 Raw cacao powder, 4 tbsp

 Rolled oats, 1¾ cup

 Maple syrup, ⅓ cup

- Blend all ingredients in food processor until mixture comes together. Shape mixture into small balls;
- Refrigerate for 1 hour before serving.

QUICK & HEALTHY
Oat Waffles

 Maple syrup, 2 tsp

 Almond milk, 1¼ cup

 Coconut oil, ⅓ cup

 Rolled oats, 2 cups

 Mashed banana, ½ cup

 Baking powder, 1 tsp

 Salt, ⅓ tsp

- To the blender, add milk, banana, oil, maple syrup, salt, baking powder and blend until completely smooth;
- Add in flour and pulse until just combined;
- Heat up your waffle maker and cook to preferred doneness.

FLAX SEED
Healthy Crackers

 Flax seeds, 1 cup

 Water, ½ cup

 Salt, ¼ tsp

 Dried rosemary, 1 tsp

 Garlic powder, ½ tsp

 Black pepper, ¼ tsp

 +

- Mix flax seeds, water, spices; Spread mixture on baking pan with parchment paper;
- Bake at 275°F (135°C) for 50 min.

BANANA
Oat Cookies

 Cacao nibs 2 tbsp

 Rolled oats, 1 cup

 Bananas, 2 large

 Peanut butter, 2 tbsp

 Protein powder, 2 scoops

 +

- Mash bananas;
- Add all ingredients; Make dough; Shape into disks;
- Bake for 15 minutes at 350°F (180°C)

PUMPKIN & CHIA SEEDS
Granola Bars

 Rolled oats, 1 cup

 Almonds, 1 tbsp

 Chia seeds, 1 tbsp

 Pitted dates, ½ cup

 Pumpkin seeds, 1 tbsp

 Sesame seeds, 1 tbsp

 +

- Blend all ingredients in food processor;
- Spread the mixture on a baking sheet;
- Bake for 15 minutes at 350°F (180°C).

SIMPLE AND HEALTHY
Nice Cream

 Raw cacao powder,
3 tbsp

 Frozen bananas,
3 large

 Blend all ingredients until smooth. Serve.

MIXED BERRY
Frozen Fudge

 Creamed coconut, 300 g

 Maple syrup, 2 tbsp

 Frozen mixed berries, 1 cup

 + ❄

- Blend all ingredients until smooth;
- Freeze for at least 3 hours to solidify.

COCONUT MILK
Blueberry Ice Cream

 Frozen blueberries,
1 cup

 Raw cashews,
1 cup

 Coconut milk,
½ cup

INTEGRAL
HEALING

 Frozen bananas,
2 medium

- Blend all ingredients until smooth;
- Freeze for 4-5 hours for soft serve and 5-6 hours for firmer ice cream.

BERRY LAYERED
Chia Pudding

TOP LAYER:

 Frozen banana ½ medium

 Rolled oats, ⅓ cup

 Raspberries, 1 cup

 Almond milk, ½ cup

BOTTOM LAYER:

 Chia seeds, ¼ cup

 Maple syrup, 1 tbsp

 Almond milk, ¾ cup

- Mix all the ingredients in bottom layer;
- Place in the fridge, let sit for 2 hours;
- Add top layer. Refrigerate for at least 2 hours.

BANANA & BLUEBERRY
Goji Ice Cream

 Goji berries (soaked),
½ cup

 Pitted dates,
½ cup

 Cinnamon,
1 tsp

 Blueberries,
2 cups

 Frozen
banana,
2 medium

 Blend and freeze for 4-5 hours for soft
serve and 6 hours for firmer ice cream.

Printed in Great Britain
by Amazon